PRETTY BRAIN

Descrierea CIP a Bibliotecii Naţionale a României
TRUTA, ANTONIA M.
Pretty brain : a collection of poetry / Antonia M. Truta. - Cluj-Napoca : Casa cărţii de ştiinţă, 2022
ISBN 978-606-17-2033-0

821.135.1

Casa Cărții de Știință
Coperta: Roxana Ardelean
Redactor: Ada Blendea
B-dul Eroilor nr. 6-8, ap. 12
Cluj-Napoca, 400129
Tel: 0264-431920
E-mail: editura@casacartii.ro

PRETTY BRAIN

A Collection of Poetry

Antonia M. Truta

Casa Cărţii de Ştiinţă

Cluj-Napoca, 2022

To Mano, my dear grandma

Table of Contents

She

She is beautiful in the most tragically fantastic way possible,

Terrifying in charm; pull; allure, melting of obscure,
surreal features
She must be art, if not its definition: horror.

Annihilating, and I know it will be, but I am helplessly only
mere mortal
Tossed around in hands of the uncaring and maniacally pretty;

Like a dream so strange, I awake from it not quite sure,
If I instead had a lovely nightmare.

Of torrent, glows of gleam; I think your eye, alone,
holds screams.
I fear she'll destroy me, all while I also scare to think that she
may just not.

Beauty is a horrid-like thing made to tremble before,
And creation is painted out more like destruction,

with its passings.

Let me be, away from she; with aura and unaffectedness

She is beautiful in the most tragically fantastic
way ever possible.

Scream

I am never satisfied with anything and it will be my downfall.
My ambitions will be my own undoing;

Like some greek tragedy that isn't even famous,
All just worry, and stresses, and irrelevancies of me.
Me, me: I can never escape myself.

Potential, potential: I am an indexed
and undecided half-truth,
With a somebody of a something still attached to my name.
I don't want to meditate, go on walks;
or simply think positively

What I want to do is scream.
Scream my throat out, scream my lungs raw;
Scream until I forget the cause, until I forget I can *not.*

What I want is to scream until I can scream no more.
Scream, scream: until there is nothing left;
of voids; of nothing left.

Cursory

Cross your legs, tie your tongue,
and wear those pretty little heels you can run in:

Where was the evil stranger, in the alley?
That dark, far, far alley;

That was supposed to be escapable,
where I was supposed to have a chance,
And wherever was the fight; the unknown;
the part of crime?

Cross your legs, tie your tongue,
and wear those pretty little heels you can run in:

It's always been men I know:
It's always been men I know.

Go Figure Out

If I cannot figure myself out,

there is no way anyone else has

If I cannot figure myself out, can I still be alive?

I may be a caricature of my mind, my memories

The false things we invent

When we want not to live scared of the true,

There is no fallen satan, there never was

The demon just waits and lies in rue

Cheri Lemonade

Hi, I am Cheri.
I am Cheri.

I like lemonade,
Bittersweet to the tongue,
Bittersweet like a soul.

I want to be able to say that kiss was null
Another meaningless wave, only abroad a hull;

You have no idea why you do what it is you do to me.

That summer, this summer, unsurely the next,
You tuck back my hair; you pluck my heart:
A musician, maliciously so.

Cherries, and strawberries, and watermelon,
And cherry. Flower. Spring of bud.
Beware, beware, I am no beauty for you,
But, no, you do not listen, ugh, you;

I like lemonade, and I like certain parts of you:
I'll snap open your unclasped heart in two;
And wait to watch the bleed.

You should have never trust me, sweet.

Look at how it all burns;
Bittersweet, like a sunset, like a soul, at the end,
Like why I so like stolen, stolen away lemonade.
The cups have not only ice bruises, but blood:

I wonder, wonder whose,

For sweethearts do have no blues.
For sweethearts do have no blues.

Lunar Eclipse

Lunar eclipse, lunar eclipse,
You are not mine:
You never once were.

Lunar eclipse, lunar eclipse,
I missed you before I knew you
You never do stay; one, two,
And the years stroll by in singles

They are whispering: know this,
The annual dance reoccurs.

I wait in glass hope for the woes to not
But they always do, they always do,
They always stay.
Unlike you; so unlike you.

Lunar eclipse, lunar eclipse,
I missed myself before I knew her;
But my heart grows old,

Goes old, and it forgets itself.

Lunar eclipse, lunar eclipse,

You are not mine:

You never once were.

Alternative Universe

Somewhere, somehow, sometime:
this life never once entwined with mine.

Please: do not ever perceive me as I ever-am,
Do no longer beset eyes upon brows
Or care to, anymore, myself, see or hear or know, now;

Still, I ask you do not yet leave.

Although we are not genuine, and our future is already history,
Still, I ask you do not yet leave.

Sit still. Not for a little bit.
For just a while, only, I promise: stay, stay.

I know, I am a hypocrite. I crave what I run from most.

And I kill my own heart for poetry,
even more so than it heals me alive,
But this life is a bore; an almost middle of nowhere,

getting nowhere anytime soon,
So being a writer is my sole escapism into romance,
and not death,
For there is no art in calculations,

Thus I want midnights, and gardens, and silks;
and every emotion ever to exist
I am sick of numbers, charts, figures;
Instead of dancing, dancing night-lorn figures.

Ah, trips all upon a trick of fake nostalgic pasts:
Unholily, unlike it, for it never does ever truly last. At all.
Only, in falls.

Somewhere, somehow, sometime:
this life never once entwined with mine.

Brother

Oh, he always was the favorite, that mongrel, that brute.
That spike of ployed innocence; a deploy,
by the one who thinks of himself as so coy,
Who shrivels into things I thought
he was taught were immoral;
By something that once, in some way represented a teacher
An experience with sway, a pain seen, an anything:
A damned considerate thought
once in a damned while would do.

I spent my childhood trying to care after you.

But, no, he was always the favorite,
he the so casually plotting demon,
The boisterous and loud without guilt; projector,
for he was never taught to minimize
Any part of himself, any things of material, any sufferings.
He who I'm sure thinks to have such perceived charisma,
is to never meet consequence.
A rude awakening will someday,

someday far too late, ensue;
Where he the end all, end be,
decidedly not merrily discovers he is but a fool.

Iron Irony

I saw an article on classism get written on wall street.

My, my, are they really so blind;
or simply insensitive and uncaring?
It may as well have turned even me, the to lied, blind.
And I guess that may have been in part, the point.

I saw an article on classism get written on wall street.

Those rich people must see struggles
as some entertaining thing,
And, oh me, oh my, please tell me this is just a lie:
isn't that the dream?
The dream, that dream, the american dream;
it was only ever truly theirs.
Not here, not there, why,
not in any a reachable an anywhere!

I saw an article on classism get written on wall street.
It was a shiny little prop, a dangling consumerist toy,

But, see, we are not like these people,
hush, hush, we cannot do these likewise things.
Can hardly see or know them, too,
for it is just to be damned, if we so do.

I saw an article on classism get written on wall street.

I worry about bills I have yet to receive,
I stress and then stress some over tuition,
The more affordable doctors all tell me to better manage my
time, to find more of it for myself. To medicate or meditate.
But, no, no, those cannot be possible for me;

I did see an article on classism be written on Wall Street.
Both are unrealistic; and I, the worker, worker, down the
hall, only have time for realism
I saw an article on classism get written on wall street.

Or so it seems: in my official office place;
not in my own dreams.
Which I think have begun to die. As I cannot remember
the last one I ever did have.
I saw an article on classism get written on wall street.

The official ones, the politicians,

try to come and talk to me again;

They talk, talk, talk like they know.

We both know that they do not.

They do not.

Lights

'If I cannot figure myself out, can I still be alive?'

Do I have any stake to the right?

The bane of my existence is my existence.
I fall in and out of half-desperate things, of love, of demise,

City after city; night after night:
the lights shake up and taunt me

They almost know I have nowhere to be.
They almost know I helplessly want to feel loved,

But that I need unconditional freedom.
See, I was not born to be of softer, more lovable flings.

And it is a so lonely thing to be sentimental and enraged, both

Oath

I worry that love may be violence,
that sin may not be found in despair;
That if I am alone, unknown, I am nothing.
And I am noting the way the what-if and whatnots track
by, drag on, snag onto the wrist of twisted time:
The veins pulse a bulged blue; with green, ivory,
vignettes of vines between,
If I reign as unloved, do I remain as unseen? A Queen:

A mangled monarch of blood
and glisten of deadly frozen snow,
There has to be something that only lovers know,

Oh, oh, I know: reciprocity, vulnerability;
The emotion as full and cool as the sea,
it must be a relief to know you have cares
And frets and someone to give, to share them to;
that one's capacity for love is used
Not tested under pressure of growth, and never release,
Running on an explosion's lease,

No clever coconspirator with needs:
I swear this loneliness is like an oath.
A pact, unsealed, not screamed,
a lover without a single dream
Of ever once being loved, quite as much or back, so,
Sew the mistrust into dew, into doe,
fearful of the unfamiliar and new: happiness,

It seems like a fog, not a bliss;
I am sure I could become lost in my idea of it:
That I am, that I half-live in its conception of delusion, that
it's a lisp of endearment to others who have known or
know its truth, its tale, anything beyond the stale fleeting,

That my pitiful words and wishes and somewhat hopes may
well seem like a child trying to make it up, up to the moon;
unfilled plastic cup,
Burbling away with science they cannot possibly make true,
but take not blue,
No, no, brake my dead red heart in an art of you.
You, monster of love, longingly, unforeseen to me,
Belonging to some part of me, you:
What? You have never once, twice, thrice, or ever
known comforting misery like I have

It becomes a fossilized home;
It crystallizes into all you know,
Threatening to strangle, but it is so familiar a feel,
that it all starts to feel like a home:
A home without a holiness, no homeliness, a dome only
with longing loneliness

An altar for yearnings and hearing of your own
Long blues, that stretch-out beyond the singings of shrieks
of any nearer undue clues,
The form that becomes you; I am married to its hidden
shadow, its irresistibility

All of the invisible, intangible, and merciless hold over me:
another oath, an engagement,
It is enraging and I fear I cannot ever leave, or have it in me
to be so, to know what it is living with a mind freed:
freed of itself, somehow.
Impossibly, surely: that I am quite unsure even exists
outside of my own head;
It, still, seems only an illusion
And I am fond of ideas but not of their spirals,
I am fond of love and not any lovers,

I am the banished one, the unseen,
The unloved and, thus, unknown; it seems.
But I refuse to beg to change any part of it.

Like a sterling steel silver dream of a dream,
It all tauntingly daunts and haunts me, me
And I am all I can care to see, to be, to know:
To love. In an oath, in any: to love.

Someone

A woman cuts an orange, a man murders six.
Every hour, of everyday. Where does that leave us?
Where does that lead us to?

I am looking at this orange, its segments, its halve, its twin
I cut it up and devour it all-whole, both.
Like I have the right.
I leave the unwanted peel to rot.

I do not know what the point of this poem is,
except that I do.
The orange is not a blood one, but it bleeds. Surrealism.

A metaphor. No, it is a nothing fruit.
I assign meaning to the mundane as though it lives to care.

Another hour passes.
I know there is nothing I can do.
The family dog sits behind the curtain,
in front of the window, watching

As always: she sees nothing before or after her.
She simply sits and waits. For what? The hot shot,
The one dot, the chance for a change

My once orange lies still in segments.
My mouth and eyes feel dry.

I think I do not want to know the point of this poem.
At this point, I think I well fear it. Maybe I already have, subconsciously.
It is too disorderly.
I, senselessly, wrote it like I had the right.

Another hour passes, by and by.

I think I am going to cry.

So I swallow all the vitamins rigidly.
They scrape on down, and feel like they do not work.
This is not a progress of anything, there is no way it can be.
My murdered orange must agree.

And I watch random videos to kill my mind, kill the time.
I know well it does not work. That it cannot.

Another hour passes. Six more.

Dear orange, dear god, this cannot be real.

Except that it is.

But the dog barks; she saw something.

Someone.

Cup of Coffee

I unfairly expect you to energize me,

Give me life, a mean; anything but an end.

And in the end,

You're only a cup of coffee.

For god's sake, mostly just a type of bean.

And I should not expect and want so much

It's killing me so, slow.

Baby Puppy

You are so tiny and innocent and cute,
With no clue:
you would not know your left paw from your right,
Or up, or down,
Or how your adorableness could, people's hearts, drown

How you are only a mess of fur with spots and those eyes,
And I love you, I love you, I love you dearly so.

You probably just want me to leave you alone,
You're tired, and do not want to put up some show

And you know you'll always be the star, anyway.
Innovative inventor, ingenue, so invincible but harmless:

Baby, puppy, you yawn with all your snout
and drowsily go off to dream.
You will never know how loved you are.
It, in part, in my heart, breaks me.

Heartaches and Cafés

Everything is coming to an end,
and I am thrilled and terrified.
Grilled and tricked,
It goes to show the relentless shift.

Of ups, ups and downtown downs,
The air of jazz in breath, in fog,
in cafe after another after one
The cafe where I became upon you:
And, dear, you were not becoming

Ruffled waves of hair and eyes of my doom,
I should've known you'd break my heart,
Your own, too, and unsurely a dozen left to seal

Slumped and handsome:
You soon held my heart for ransom,
Nothing about this was ever sober.
Swoon, and powerful prose does that, all;
Theatrics always stir people up a little,

Good action, but though you do it so wrong,

You stay long enough to do it, still;

you get up every single day,

With every single say: and you choose to stay.

To me, to we. To ushered out us.

Winter Tree

Droops of claws that tangle and stream,
In small, small flicks that scream.
Dreadful and dead frames:
Lined in petrol,
Hollows of attack and pity, both
Gripping hands of want of cold winter trees,
Bark all begging and crisply dying or dead
Dark muck pooled, still, below:
Sightless and motionless and unending.
With somethings hidden within, beneath,
Of the unsure, or unknown, or unbecoming
Sprouted frozen sticks,
Rounded off in clips,
By the chipped of above or deep:
Crevices and cracks and stickily tears
Silent but all-knowing in sap;
Not keen, cannot, do not, ever see:
Bearing witness to no wooden travesty
Of selves and all,
Glued together only by yuck,

To the dirt of the so loathed ground:
Wants to move in freedom ring, but who
Who does know how to, anymore?
They hardly exist, the trees;
Dreary mulberry mildew things,
Do they know hate and whatnot, what else?
Rigid bones of wood,
Nearly crack to strangle all:
A violent beauty of the not benevolent.

Apocalypse

The apocalypse had no horsemen or wide, shadowing doom:
It had me, and you.
The sky still stayed blue, the clouds did not vanish into an
abyss of ash
No sirens rang; no devils sang;
there was no hip-holster or stash,
There were no cargo pants, or guns, or wandering groups.
There was only silence and unspoken tokens.
And everyone knew.
Some, the rich, flew; the rest wallowed.
We were too young. We were the first to be swallowed.
There was nothing I could do, to save you.
It was my last thought:
Maybe, a revenge of a revolutionary
Was something to be sought:
That I should have set it all, while I still had the chance.
Together, now, forever, now, our bones still dance;
And laugh, laugh at the stuff of our dooms.
What else was there to possibly do?
I never could have saved you, you or the world.

For nothing is ever like in the films;

Art only imitates itself, life always imitates death.

Art only imitates itself, life always imitates death.

Honey-Lovers

As sweet as honey, sting of my heart, bee my Valentine:

Once a lover, always a lover,
I'm finding that no one can ever really leave me.
Not when her, his; your image floats in all I see and touch
I miss knowing you. So much.

And I fear I will never forget;
For I am not the one who leaves an indifferent member,
I am forced to be the one unremembered.

You've glued yourself, selves, to me like bees
To honey: but an icky stick; in time, makes me only sick so.

Keen Butterflies, Bitter Kerosene

There are butterflies in my stomach and they are eating up and tearing out the lining.

Sometimes, I am so relentlessly alive, I feel paralyzed;
I am so alive, it feels dead.

My heart is tired. And my mind has, long, been broken.
Please, leave them both be: this is my plea

Butterflies soon spiral out into tornadoes,
Their mutated mutant wings only a perpetuate propeller,
Is there beauty and pain, both, in the storm?
Unrequitedly so.

But it does not take very long before love begins to hurt.
If this nightmare is love.
Churning and turning, it kills and kills me to the bone.

Yet, still, this haunts me, and it haunts me;
And I am disgruntled and undecided of everything.

Bitter butterflies in my belly, fueled, so fueled:

tearing out its lining, outlining nothing.

Traveler's World Body

Traveler, traveler: in a world, a body of it, say:
I am restless for travel, and I never once felt to feel at home.
New York has my soul. Cairo can have my hands.
Venice, my eyes.

Traveler, traveler: in a world, a body of it, say:
The world: my toy, my oyster;
If this were in some sunset film.
Feeling and flowing and loving and living
would all seem so easy

Traveler, traveler: in a world, a body of it, say:
London can have my charm. Paris, my wink.
My hometown:
Romanian city, my heart, Cluj-Napoca, my heart.
I'll let Toronto and Montreal at my rumble.

Traveler, traveler: in a world, a body of it, say:
Give my buzz away to Tokyo,
my idle ideas to San Francisco.

My tired and pink cheeks to Seoul.

Traveler, traveler: in a world, a body of it, say:

Let me know what it is, how it feels, to be alive

Let me be all of these people and none at all:

Let me live before I die.

Traveler, traveler: in a world, a body of it, say:

I can't stay in this flatland, so had, still sad, sitting,

place much longer.

I'll visit once I've had a long break, and long after,

Traveler, traveler: in a world, a body of it, say:

But I need to see the world, and I need to see it all alone,

And I do not want any of that which I can actually have;

Any ambitions that are beyond a wish, a will,

No, no, I seem to want to know the world.

I seem to want the world.

Places

So long, so long, you lumbered up something of a song:
I am forlorn when I am with; and without you

Any place I am, when I am around you,
is the most beautiful I have ever seen:

And there, therein lies the problem,
See, I have no one to dedicate that line to.
I feel like I should,
I feel like love poems may need a recipient;

Other than uncaring moons and bottled swoons
I emote, dote, quote so much and say, express, so little.
Oh, yes, I am one out to impress.

Me and my pen; my weapon, my life, my work-medium,
All I have and all I know. None to show.

I fear all my poetry of love may never have a recipient;
I fear I am well-wasting my own damned time.

Any place I am, when I am around you,
is the most beautiful I have ever seen:

What a linen-lovely line, with only emptiness behind.

A Numbness

The flowers:

They are dead,

The ocean engulfs the only land we've ever known,

Whole skies have ignited into flames

And the disciple has become despicable:

The mighty have all fallen dead,

Love is found out to actually only be obsessive dread.

Irony and coincidence: lie.

And, lies: to be true.

But the meaning to and in the storm,

The conclusion hidden within the chaos,

Is turned over. Revealing nothing:

No answer at all.

It is not a surprise.

It always was a nothingness in experiences.

Pity-Things of Heart

Love me as though you hate me:
like we, too, can be of the dreadful and divine

I can pin-point our start;
the many of the looming, rued, roomful lot.

A bright red sweater, a wide eccentric smile,
a curious head tilt:
The sweetness of her shyness, the debonair mystery of his air
At this rate, I just love the idea of love.

I would like a negate of this negative, the anecdote of dotes,
if one will

But you are true, and truly perfect, and tyrannical in
that perception, are

You have intricately stricken me moonstruck and, sickened,
we mooned.
Offer the unknowns of it all, to our hearts' heard wounds

They drool and bleed;

we devour the uncut, unkempt, unkept pity-things.

Invincibly

I write to lay things to rest, do not
take acknowledgment as compliment.
For my rhymes are half-tombstone to half-emotion.
Lord knows, I am desensitized to feel
It all, wholly or Holy;
Nor do I have the rights, stakes, the brakes.
Or break. Straw. Reason:
So called, method to madness.
Only can I claim results to the invincible pops of whirls
that happen.
Only can I cry in my dreams;
In a space, outside of time.
A space of mad spasm, mine. No refine.
Or refrain, restrains, to it all.
Unholy; invincible so.

I write to lay thing to rest, do not
take acknowledgment as compliment.
For my rhymes are half tombstone to half emotion, withal.

A Romantic's Conversation

"No, no, I am a black cat. A broken mirror," I droll, "You
cannot want me."

One cannot accompany the romantic without courting their own destruction

"A poet. Oh, but how I do." Hope winks in response;
Ever the optimist in faces and places of doom, Destiny
drinks and nods along at her shoulder, adding on:
"It's true. I am the inevitable. I would know."

"Ah, so Love is not of choice. At all?" I mumble with a
sigh. "I hoped it so, I think it so."

Destiny darkens at this. "I never had any! Any love, any
choice, a say. Any no, a 'nay.' I've been fixed, transfixed,
ascending into doom for all of time. I am the one who
should sigh; I am the one to mourn for.
I am the one who lives dead."
"Pretty line, pretty head." Hope blurts out, words slurred.
In-between meanings, blurred.

"Does none of this make sense?" she laughs; quieter, then,
Hope says: "Perhaps it is not quite meant to. Only idiots
happily dine, never whine. Perhaps I, I am finally lost."

"Or, perhaps," I pipe up, "I may be the invisible one, actually. Unseen,
unknown. The romantic: so romantically alone."
I puff air, an almost-laugh, continue on:
"Gods, I romanticize even the misery.
Like it needs a feel; a motive of song, to make sense;
to be really real."

Destiny, tsk, "Assigning logistic to eternal emotion? Darling,
it never ends well."
Taking a swell swig, Destiny details:

"Oh, no, darling, no, that always all goes to hell. The things;
to the separate rings. Circles of circles. Realities to realities."
She stops, looks over at me. Sees the gleam.

"You cannot know more. You cannot want more. That,
Romantic, is your problem: you refuse to not dream."
A smile, an unlikely wink: Destiny deduces:

My droll black cat; my broken mirror, one cannot accompany the destined and the romanticism without courting their own
destruction

I wake up in a sweat.
Tell myself it was all, only, a dream; another,
But I still smell the bar alcohol and contradiction.
And sense the lost, along-lost Hope.

Of The Second

I hate the number of two, I do,
Because it is exactly, always what I have been

It mirrors: not quite there, not quiet enough,
Never the choice; barely only an option,

No one has ever willingly wanted me back.
In friendships, all relationships, almost romances;

Almost a lot of things, sings,
I am always the almost.

The second.
The what-if or would-be, if not the last.

Oh, I'm the last one on the sidewalk,
I'm the closest to the street

I am the interrupted, I am the talked over,
Two-petal and bad-luck clover.

I wonder if people can even see me;
I have for all my life.

And no one ever has wonder for me,
And no one has ever cared for me,

For if someone has fallen for me;
Whatever be, they may have to be insane, I think.

Unhappy

Let you hear of my epiphany, the latest,
that only idiots are happy.

Literarily, and literally.
But I often see this giddiness and childish glee within them,
And, god, I wish I were natively naive again.

One day of insanity is rewarded only with another

And, so, I breathe an endless end down this preposterous path.
Fruitless mere existence; mediocrity; and persistence

I have a fervor to be feral, to forget it all and live fabulously,
But I fear that was never for me.
I was not one made to be happy,
I don't think I would know how to be.

One day of insanity is rewarded only with another
And I was not one made to be happy,
I do not at all think I would know how to be.

Sucker

I sawed off my hair like I gave a care, like I had anything
left in me to give.
This is not a love poem.

So, the scissor saws and claws away at the strands;
And no one did know or care.
Now or then, no one ever seems to
Or ever does, to do so would be anew; a not nothing,
a but sludge. All I feel.

For you, you: I almost do.
My dearly illicit, bothersome pew.
I vow to haunt the crevices that hand left behind,
Oh, I won't be another fond little memory
to play with and love, leave, and live without:

Not me. No; no. Me: I make men miserable.
Say, I even make them pay

All I do is exist and, my god, my good lord,

how ghastly is the sight;

How unmanly the light,
as I strangle and wrestle with the among
Yes. I love on but I live on to spite.

I cannot bring myself to understand destruction,
No woman of word, I am a girl, undirected and uncontrolled:
Ah, I must be unhinged, also.
Unlike you, ugh, you, I was seemingly sane and still am so,
but swear to me to be blue;

It'll be easier for us both, darling;
Sweet, sweet misery. I warn, I yearn, I yawn:
do not make me hunt to haunt you.

Political

They say I am angry, swear above all I am crazy,
But who is it who made me so;
molded the rotten-up yeasted dough?

Things always seem to look more beautiful in motion, in
life,
And everything about me feels so stagnant.

But what can I do, what do I do with all this anger?
Where can I set down this relentless rage?
Am I bound to it; is it a segment of me,
What is this shadow showing? Why can't I, it, see?

Have I been blinded, have I blinded myself;
It was fine, so fine up until it wasn't
Everything just makes sense until it unjustly doesn't;
It is like the clicks have unclogged,
the machine has materialized.
It has been broken, yolked, mocked;
It cannot go on, beaten down, like this.

Alive, alive, but at what hellish sin of a cost?
I cannot go on, beaten down, like this.

To myself, even, I hardly seem human: look
at what I have become,
Bluffs about buffs and tough and rumble steel,
Dried, piercing, cottoned thing of a voice, of shards, of pity

Oh; all I know is politics,
In the struggle of an eye; in the life of but a life.

And I am very angry, sworn to be crazy,
But dare not to stare at who it was, what it is
that made me so.
No, no: no foul crawl of a reek likes a mirror.

Anguish

How much longer must I anguish?
My skin is brittle as sandpaper,
My eyes: pools of doe pain,
All I feel anymore is pain or numb, numb…

It's always rain, it's always rain,
I do love the rain; actual rain,
But that type never comes often enough.

I, in part, want to compact my life into pretty little words
So I don't have to deal with all this rage.
And all of its own rage, its rages, upon my stage.

I know, now: no one is coming to save me,
And no one was ever there. I must anguish, languish onward.
No one is coming to save me…

I: Maternal

The beekeeper's daughter is my mother;
And the writer's daughter, the poet's daughter,
the nurse's daughter.
Then the engineer's wife; the children's mother.

Mom, mom: did you ever have anything of your own?
Was I the substitute, the cloy,
a decoy thing of a different daughter
I want to know, did you feel used; torn through; alone,
You pass it generationally like a loan.
And I have not the heart to hurt in front of you,
I thought maybe a cutaway gutsy diary would do.
No cutesy little clue did you ever offer,
No solution or glue: I was special to abuse, to throw about,
To yell at when nothing else was around;
When I was the daughter, the present, the ever here.
My mother saw the true, the new: so I was for slew:
Mom, to you, the dried and dreaded dream
Your first lesson was no woman makes it out okay.
The possibility, the potential; I just had to be stamped, too,

How dare I so represent you.

After you already cut my carcass out to,

Then criticized the made-model saint

You squeeze and almost strangle the

same places I know you hate.

What if it was identity, personality, that I shut up and ate;

Your influence was almost too late to catch:

Tried to make me feel also invisible, I think,

The other broken one on another brink

One to coddle into control;

To fake out, to puncture to leak, eek, to lie to,

To break and break and silence the unholy, unworthy beak of me

Did you see this, truly think this, as love?

II: Paternal

Of course I could love you before I knew what you were,
who you were.
Before I could see without the influence of your shadow,
Over anything, over everything,
over all I could possibly even try to see:
You never let me forget; lived to remind
I used to think you were a hero before I knew better;
The frustration has a warp of its own.
A throw of confusion, a twisted pulse of rage,
I lived like I was made in your cage
No bird, only wired rat, dead with smell;
and inconvenient, for that,
But you insisted otherwise. I was only some bug to you.
Manageable, controllable: dad, I don't know which of us is
more scared of the other.
And another another fight,
more screaming and yells and tear, tears,
So do go on the years: bleeding,
And I try to rationalize and conceptualize this reality,
as though I care to can,

Anymore; look at the score, the rotten decomposed core
All the things I worked for are all for nothing;
are never enough,
I feel I never knew you: only the demise, the despise.
Devil father, do not bother, I know you would hate this;
Let alone, that it was not the first work, not the original idea.
Your terrifying aryan eye, dead-bright in its blue,
Shines for I am, still, sometimes scared of you.
And I used to be so, me, the pushed about tower, the closest
lumber tree;
No life, or hug; the roach, the bug, always the unwanted one.
The ignored or berated daughter of you,
paraded about like artifact on occasion;
I thought the pupil stupid and I craved it the same;
Evil, evil, you are to blame; unlike anything
else wretched, ever.
The last name does not feel like mine, it is a swine,
it was never shared.
It was burned onto me: I cannot beat it,
can hardly think of its weight,
To somehow escape, or run from, it cannot be done;
against all my hopes, my years.
And fears; look at what I am, who I am,
At least, once, see me before you neglect again.

Ex-Friend, Ex-Friend

Hardly breathe, hardly speak, hardly dare to feel for fear

Of you, and your big emotion; your huge control;
your large, choking scope

I never told you that you made me despair so

I actually wish you all the worst,
I hope your dreams all haunt you
I hope you awake to messes, and catastrophe, and nothing
but inconvenience
That you sleep only from tears;
sleep without any peace, at that
I dare you to apologize to me
Now, I would tear you apart into scraps

I dare you to dare be happy, after what you have done to me
You've filled my mind with rage and lies
about what the past was like
You must think it all so cheery,

All the while you sashayed and sauntered in your rot,
I hardly escaped the claws of you

I know it was a spanned operation, it took me much time:
My heart wanted to believe you
Perhaps you know what I mean;
I think you may have once had one, too
After it all, I was always still the issue

By damnable everything, all I did was love you

My heart wanted to befriend you
To help you, before I knew you
were simply born an idiotic wrecker
You reek of evil meanness, of foul wretch,
I hope our memories die and you live as just a mediocre mess

I feel wonderful knowing I've already surpassed you

Black Coffee with Vanilla

Black coffee with extract of vanilla
It is an interesting combination;
And I am trying to decide what it represents
But it agrees not, cares not for my frets or poetics

The English teacher says I am convoluted, choppy
I cannot say I disagree;

Like I cannot say I have a way with words
Rather: I think words have always had their way with me

The candles sit on my desk, burnt and silent
There is no emotion in their invisible dance
I hope my writings stand a, one, some chance
I hate to think them only more scrawls

Or more scratches, more unwanted refuse
I toss out nothingness and deliver it with silver gusto
And as I am a nameless, I have no exact brand
No style or one thing to uphold;

For I am only untold

Ah, that is it: I am only this black coffee with extract of vanilla

If it sounds pretentious, it is because: it is

Symbolically, I bitterly glue myself intact and end with an ache

There is nothing original I can ever make:

I am a copy of what I've loved

A hint, a tinge, a pinch of sweet tint in the flavor

And then the dry, bitter caffeine:

To think, that is the energizing part

Ironic how all is fueled by corrupt taste

Yet I am scared to express too much, too,

I think this; and I feel that; and my brain is a riffraff tat

I water down thoughts into subjective sentences

To avoid seeming too big, too bulky, too threatening in mind

Now, why do I do it? Why can I not stop?

Some part is entrained in me, is me;

Makes up the shadows of what-if's and if-only's:

I feel that, in me, those may just be true

But I should move on

I know that, although it is a so insufferable thing to know,

As most pleasantries are.

Nightingale's Talk

To define, to limit: I am simply an enigma
I am the night
I am beyond your mortal words and worlds,
I am indescribable yet real
What I am, is hypocrisy
And you cannot understand me for as long as you live
I will change, day after day, to keep you from me
I despise commitments
I cannot heal my wings of hate here

At Twelve O' Five

At twelve and five, the birds lie dormant
The late showers may sing
Ears ring onward and on, upon nothing
And over the sluggish afternoon haze

The day is barely over by a slight,
One has made it out
At five beyond twelve, there is no more fight
Only the willows still swing now

At twelve and five, the worms cry formant
The fate bowers say king
Fears ping off-word and of, up on noting
And cover the mulish under-swoon daze
The bay is hairily under by a sight,
Done are forbade pouts
At five beyond twelve, there is no more light
Only the willows still swing now
Only the willows still swing now

One Bite

This loneliness is going to eat me uncut,

Longing is going to eat me uncut

It'll savor not devour me, I see

This is all so unforgiving

Every body talks

Everybody talks to hear themselves talk;

To use words as decorum,

My precious words:

As flourish to otherwise nonsense

Everybody talks

And talks of feeling alone in a crowded room,

At that

How romantic and tragic the image is

I feel most unloved when surrounded

By others who are supposed to love

What of to feel crowded with nothingness?

What of the marble trapped saints?

Sun and Sea

The sun rises over the sea:
Reflecting but not seeing, waves move to its light,
clouds dare not to appear
It is bright, it is only a start.
I am a half-baked thing,
No one knows what to do with me
Least of all, me
There are books and articles and the like
Advice columns and art issues;
But what can encapsulate this not whole weight,
this half-empty muck?
Can anything?
The words may be lost in numbers,
As bumpers are lost on streets,
As the days, days, days are lost on me
I feel like a badly fleshed out idea
There is proof of concept but is is inky and unsure of itself,
There is possibility
Though it is strangling and cannot be wrangled together
Together or apart, the sun and sea,

They both are still relentless

Stuck in routine, trapped in time,

If they could feel, would they scream?

Would they feel they had the right?

Could-Cannot

I could love the world for all it was worth,
I could throw my heart upon every sword
and cry joy at every stupid sunrise and sunset
But that is not what I am
The truth: the truth is, it was a force
that kept me alive for so long
For all of those eons
I am not quite sure what has kept me here
Maybe human stubbornness,
Maybe I will always inherently fight
I cannot go
I cannot set down my pounding heart, my tense veins, my air

Unforgotten

Dead people once walked, sang, talked, breathed, bathed

Among the dirts we now still feed
Life feels sore, like back muscles that pang
With a deadbolt snap
With harsher hard rugs about to snag

I remember I want to tell you something
Or I think of a joke
But then I remember you are gone and there is no one to tell
I don't know if I knew you well

Specific Misery

My food tastes cold and my eyes are not in focus

It cannot get worse,

Please, it cannot get worse,

I suggest hangouts and movies I cannot even go watch

I am destroying myself for nothing but I cannot stop

My mother worries about how much coffee I drink

My poor system,

Pumped with caffeine like a solution

Pain is white hot

I feel the desperate anger better poets describe

Halos

The ambience is poetic
This is bliss

I am in a space outside of time where every color seems
like painted dawn
Vaguely, not loudly
Everything is young and bouncy
Gleeful, joyous things are around me
I want wind on my face and sun on my hips, like this, again

Innocence and humanity and pureness
Is here and ever near
Is in telling there is something, a little something just there,
A little over,
On someone's eyelashes

My heart forever bats on

Down

Like a greek tragedy that isn't even famous,
I have no salvation
Only demonic dragons
And breaths of flames, of fire
I don't want to keep up this fight
I am sick of killing to stay alive

I only wish so much that someone would care
That another would bother to cry over my sorrow,
Tears all fortunes for me
I'm sick of being alone
But I'm more terrified to be known

Not everything is meant for poetry
And I cannot reconcile that
If I cannot label something into words,
Cannot rhyme or describe it,
It sickly eats me alive
Every time

Lovesick

If I am lovesick, it is in an opposite sense

I'm sure I've written this before,
I am in love with the idea of love
And that is the most hard, horrid way to love any love
Maybe if I keep writing love, repeating love
I'll come to know one of my own

I court emptiness like a sweetheart
Like an art, it is in my movements I persist
Perused by doom, my smiles offer no loom
Flirtatious and traitorous:
I play them in a fuddle, like a scrabble
The manic twos
To think they compete and glare at the other
I know I have won
However, sole

No Guardian

If there were angels,

From up on some swing,

My guardian one would sing:

You come up with ideas and ideas and ideas

That you never flesh or sketch out

You design things for books you do not write

And you know how I am right

And you cry

You cry too obnoxiously, too loudly:

You cry like you can

Scratch

And you feel like you're secretly terrible,

Like you've stolen creatures or killed things

Do you deserve an epilogue;

A monster who cannot recognize itself?

Do you refer a reality, do you infer inferiority?

A bride in a little black dress is less sleek

Than the pawing, pawing great cats of doubt

Plea

All frenzied lists and tired eyes,
I am my busyness
I am my ambitions and stresses
I forgot what else there is
Help me feel really alive
Anyone, please

I know how it is, we all want to be mysterious
I know how it is, things just never change

And, about lovers and all the stereo terror
They do unto one another
Steel hearts and imaginary men,
I don't need someone to inflict whatnot onto me

I hate the feeling that I want something
I cannot stand that I have desires beyond logics
I just want more simple torment,
If not newness of life

Question-Less

Endless screaming void

Why is everything work and pain and numbness
Can I not live
Can I not breathe in peace
What is my issue;
Most people can grow to love most people,
If treated well enough for long enough:
What on Earth can be so wrong about me
Can't I get away with seeing some heart

I am only some idiot, with arms outstretched,
Asking for love
But if I got it, for whatever crude reason,
I doubt I would know what it looks like

I've been so loveless,
I wouldn't know if I was loved
So the paradox stands: I may be,
But does it matter if I do not feel it

Contradiction in a Not Rhymed Poem

I want to be alone and I want to be loved.
I'm always looking for the next story
while being stuck in the past.
I don't understand what to do with myself.
I don't think anyone sees me, I think I'll feel like this forever.
I forgot how to be myself, I cannot grasp my childhood.
I'm so tired of fighting but it's all I can do.
I run on coffee, and bad sleep, and worse memories.
I cannot focus on today.
I do not know how to relax.
I am forever chasing.
I have got to stop loving like this.
It is eating me whole and it is invisible and I am not fine,
I am only so silent because what can I say
when no one will look me in the eye.

Blue Heart

The heart is a muscle enveloped in a sac of nonsense,
I should've known to trust it not:
It promises strength, yet bends weakly

Swayer, swayed, a swath of lie
Dreadful bloodied thing; pumping and struggling for nothing

For me, allegedly, but I am naught
I am a pretty and yawning void.
I am the yet decoded, yet understandable

May swell live destined to be alone
For it is all I know, all I manifest,
All I can ever dread to resemble or be
Thrash and slash, does the heart have strings?
It can be used, it is unthinking

Now, loyalty and royalty don't coincide;
The blue rue is only dark unless shed
My mind must be trying to kill me, it directs my heart, still:

I know I am not irreparable, but I feel like it
I suppose that might be my problem:
I love, love, and love things until they make me sick
I am a waste of space, a potential of a potential:
Do not hold your breath on me.

I want to thank my heart for beating on and on,
But the pangs hurt when they hit my chest
I warn, my heart, blue, do not waste your blood on me

Ariel

I rise like a spirit,
Like the deep green sea
Far from me, far, yes, is the paradise so keen
It parrots the tale
Corroborates the call, my fall
For it and for everything
Naiveté is an unbecoming look on me

I wallow and bubble, dumbly innocent,
Unaware of all humanity has in store
I am a terribly young thing
And I have only arisen to consciousness late
The waves billow and salt me like a grate
I think I may be off-putting
In this state, in such grace of fear,
I must look wild like this; out here; like I am
But the seaweeds even cannot tangle to stop me
The slippery eel poses no match,
Nor does the scorching sun or tongues of poisonous fish
Should such things dare to exist, near

I wretch my body up upon the sand
I have made the trip
Made it swimmingly,
By the sea, I stand and scream and yell
The yellow cocoons about do not haunt me
And the sky is clear and blue, here,
And all is well, all is well.
I rest, laugh, muck about as I please
Nothing can endanger or panic me now
I have set afire the ocean tight bonds
I have no bounds, no wound up wanders,
I explore and learn at will
No cruel waters can thrash me, reach me
I am stable, I have made it above

I… Am Glum

I've lost myself, debauched myself,
I've stolen and stolen and killed.
Something, surely,
But do not ever ask me what:
I doubt I could converse anymore;
I doubt I can exist,
Everything is mechanical and surreal
Am I alive, am I a person?
I feel like a crumpled, confused nothing.
Tragedy flows and follows like a prayer,
I must be free if I live so restlessly
I *must* be free if I am always so alone
But the sky saunters on, the wind whistles along,
Only I am frozen in the throws of time,
Only I am the show that does not go on.
Everything else is moving, outside,
Things are bright and covered in light
And it overwhelms me to be alone in aloneness
I do not understand why I cannot let go,
Why I cling onto nothing

And fight tooth and nail for something I cannot see,
Against something I cannot see
I cannot understand this oath.
I cannot see what is here, I cannot hear what I am,
I feel incapable of being an anything.
I might be sad, but I forgot to keep that up,
I may unwell be unstable or a naught;
I think I am only nothing.
I do not feel present, I do not feel at all,
Selfishness is a virtue; but it has eaten my heart.
There is still yet let residue to devour,
If I am still bleeding out.
I am hopelessly stuck in traps I cannot make out,
I am fumbling and flawed and without use.
And I fear I've hurt myself beyond repair;
How do I save myself from myself;
How do I stake anything if I don't know how to be whole
I cannot be great, but I must be.

A Fullest Potential

Everything is about a fullest potential
But I am exhausted, I am extinguished,
I am ashes lazily blown in worn wind:
The destruction must be over now.
All that remains is numbness and quiet

And it is a strange peace, misery
Flashily offering reprieve and consumption both,
Daring to take the soul of something but
To leave the body and heart
But it, itself, never leaves

I've not known a more insistent love,
And I've fallen in love with everything

Everything is about a fullest potential,
A beat and a thrum and hope, hope,
But that is not the ail

I am falling apart, and I keep falling apart;

It never ends, never stitches to mends
Only ribbons out and on
The consistency is my constant hell.

It is only an ideal of potential,
Nothing full or tangible; that is its tang
Delusion and expulsion both

I am imploding, and all which is around me is exploding,
The frames are gummed fragments,
Like glass shards that have not the courtesy to even be real

Say, the doleful and the dull have a feel;
A cloudless gray, a bitter and great steel, a throwaway heart
Tossed dream, tears' gleam, ripped seam:
Love, these are all poetic symbols.
These are all dominoes of melancholy.

And I am perpetually falling to rock bottom;
All steady, all broken, all pale with ails

Never just breaking or giving up already,
I trudge and budge on; stubborn as cowards, as cattle,
As in, I am enormously unimportant.

I cannot give up, however much I may want to
Something will simply not let me;
Conscious, soul, guilt, spirit, grit, want, need.
Hope is damning: I do not understand why I still have it.

For I am a romantic though I do not know why

I've not known a more insistent love,
And I've fallen in love with everything.

Empty Romantics

Come, we here are the empty romantics
Always around, a melody of a melody of a sound,
We are the drawling and abhorred.

We are misery's room and board,
The lovely and despised;
The bright, bright and unseen.

No one here has anything but a dream,
A heart, a pocket or a penny or two
This is nowhere to belong;

It is a dome, not a home
The jumpers and pajamas and papers are strewn about;
Anybody in love, loves to think themselves a poet

But those posers are far
See, they lie in makeshift heavens
With their sweethearts and booze-like eyes,

Accompanied by something an awful lot like fearful regret

Do not worry, that vignette is not this place

There is nothing to lose, no thing to steal from the empty

On People

I wish I could prod at people like they were bones.
Crack a mind like a cantaloupe;
My "aha's!" a knife sharpened of knowledge,

A fastened soundness,
Could I see through things as if piles of ash
Were their roof and substance both.

For sheens always shine and dreams always reel on and on,
Again: all I feel is scarcely, soaringly unreal
It seems to almost click but never does the final tick

Clocks are tricks; pretty, albeit counting times
The times no one quite understands until
they are already gone

People would be feeble if we were less destructive.
Is that what keeps us alive; the deaths of things

Ode to Art

Painter's doom, trapped in a room,
A colorful tomb of melodramatics

The oils glisten like they can hear, see,
Like the landscapes have flown above this dimension
The modernism: as silent as the monk
And, by ungodly god, the post-modernism is worse

Artists are forever chewing
Ever waiting and ignored and deplored and poor,
Art has a very, very worrisome brow about her.

Lone and Wolfed

All is tired, cold, wearisome, dreary
Each year: it snows less and less upon the ears of trees;
the eerie
And, dear, the tides only grow higher, higher
What is the bleary point of a church, a squire, any lord?

I turn to writing like most turn to prayer
The ideology of the poet's philosophy is this:
If I can get it down, I can get it out
If I can get it down, I can get it out
The what or who; the sustaining substance;
remains an unknown
An invisible variable to the most alone,
There is no beauty in screaming benignity
Only a state of obvious indignity in a looping, looped present

For the religious have their witches;
Their stone sins, their resent,
As the politicians live by slogans, by campaigns,
Even devils dare to hold each other and their own

Yet: I, I have the abhorred world
A copy of a copy of a once saint,
My every victimized mirror reflects back turmoil and wrinkle

I am a debauched ingenue, if any
A cacophony of yearning hungers haunts me,
Cocooned dreams stir and awake
Eyes shut open, clamped to the outside, sealed to the deal
And slewed, swindled, all the more
What does anything worthwhile have in store;
If not lonesome fangs?

Salt

Stranded, I lay abandoned at seas: it is a day I do not know.
I dreamt I saw a paradise last night.
Really, I thought I did.

It had fruits, lush trees, set tables, light, flowers,
And land, land, land.
Hear, I believe I am having hallucinations
It might be the sun;
Or the air here;
Or the slipping sanity, about.

These waves are so unrelentingly real,
Always: they pull me back, back
They do remind and mock
It is a niche thing to daydream in waters
To be able to doze away, when so threatened so

So, the waves remind and mock and wave
But they do not abandon; they do care
If only to destroy.

Of The Bleached

With your diet sodas and beach waves,
Do you have a single worry?
I bet you don't fret.

I bet you don't really think about much beyond the moment.
Oh, and you don't know the hunger of dreams;
not like I, not like me,
The other another one you pretend not to see
For I know you cannot ignore me: I am the ugly twin,
The encapsulation of what is a detested,
loathsome thing to you

New, new, all shiny and paraded;
Shiny and shiny, all paraded anew
How treasured, and real, and alive you must feel;
I doubt you stew or are aware it won't last
Every fleeting thing is confetti for you,

Your mild moods are easy;
no brooding or sad thoughts follow you,

For you handle grace with an eye roll,

You do not care for the agonized or the onslaught,

And I am sure you write no poems.

I am sure you passively think a thought.

Abagail Penelope Meribeth

I've got a brain like fretting and fainting Victorian lady
Like I'm ruffled over high tea or,
dear me, the latest gossip papers
And I've grabbed my skirts in hand,
Maneuvered my corseted body away
from gentlemen trappers,
And out of the door, then down the street,
This London town is old but that will *not* stop me
My petticoat and I are measly and determined
I huff on, clutching the little feather puffs of my hat,
And stomp, stomp, stomp in my heeled boots
I ignore the hoots; or throw back a wink as I pass on my way
Around the sophisticated corner,
I meet with an equally frenzied friend
And I discuss how oh-so scandalized I am by it all
Before a tantalizing, graceful fall
My gown accompanies the act;
the clouds a director to the scene
Even the witnessing squirrels roll their tiny eyes
The cobblestone street catches me

I lie very theatrically, a statuette, a figurine

I awake to a yet more high-brow caller and to affairs of teas

And I've grabbed my skirts in hand.

From A Choppy, Young Roamer

Standing bright and tight and feral,
The summer I met you was the summer I died

I doubt, still, if I knew you
I think I do or do not and try

Our liaisons stretch out like limbs in the sun,
The thoughts of fear or slog are gone

Whoever you are, I love you

You are always pretty, always right
The summer I met you was the summer I died

Loving someone may mean trying to ease things for them
Living for someone means only a million self deaths

How sugary it was to ruin it all,
I have no regrets about madness of fun

The Surrealist Era

My head feels heavy
The streetlights are all too much the same
I wonder if anyone ever cared for me; I wonder if they noticed
what I am
I piece the puzzle of, yes, they did, that is why they left
Dear skylights: if this is life then what is oblivion

No one much loves me,
So, I live for nothing but the little
The overlooks
The lies
I am wasted and razed with every old tale of a new day

The bright and dangling eyes of trees
have a classic ringing to their tones,
All the way of how a forest can haunt; haunts me
Dirtied puffs stick out from the earth,
as in they too are trying to escape:
An expressionist birth of something almost fake
Uncomfortably, everything pure lays away with this view

The others' brooches reach out to half-hug, so smug,
But the pits of birches do not mind
They have the time, they are not mortal and are the time;

Everything unholily pure is there on Earth,
And if that prophecy is true
Then what the hell is hell
Lilts of jaws are deceiving, breathing, sweating out
The arts are hardly receiving
Every thing narcissistically reflects back itself

Drab

Silence is all ears to my music,
And the jagged yawp is brutal
My notes have begun to consume me
I fear myself as I never have;
I fear my own body more than I fear men's

Everything
The swabs, the personhood, the discombobulated innocence
A swap of sounds, of resignations, all not echoed
I am scared I've lost myself before I have even existed

I wish I could work normally
Without compulsivity and fusses and distractions,
And free of those little twists in my heart
Who live, as I, to yearn
For more, for better, for far:
Always, always it seems we want what we cannot have
Take absolutely anything in sight, as an example

The sphere of my want would worry me

If it wasn't so desperately beating, so fiery, so known
People are undoubtedly born for something
The issue is my heel is my mind
My life's callings:
Are to hunger, fight and to love, yearn
I am just another polarity; and tired of it, at that
For once,
I want to peer at a something and know that I can survive it;
I want to do this without ever having to kiss its ugly,
sore-ridden face

I have not fallen from grace if I never had any to start with

I am running, poorly, from a being I cannot see;
Sometimes, I try to escape this feeling only begrudgingly:
It curls up with me
Holds me, like love or happiness or other people
never care to do
That is the truth

An Elaboration

On: 'I am scared I've lost myself before I have even existed'

How do I justify myself to myself?
Can I?

When I born, I died a little
It's happened on every day since;
I was young, I am young, I am young,
But I never knew childlikeness

I am such a half-witted mess,
That my laundry rolls its buttons at my teary eyes;
My mirror sighs with every bloodshot look;

My life, a procrastination of death
And my loves, all one-sided and unspoken

If this is the case, the poisonous trace, the matted trick,
Then what reasoning can I have to exist

What right; what virtue

What home?

Aphrodite

Acknowledge how I am a goddess

Make me your example, make me your cross,
Put me up as the moon among the stars

Can you quiet for me a moment;
Can your heart stutter at my eyes and whims?

Let me know you love me, let me be the one to leave
Treat my every word like an altar
My flower bands, crowns for a queen

It is a simple thing, to obsess

Offer me everything, honor your vow
Never once dare to stray, curse, or get lazy

Brew tea and watch as I break hearts,
Knowing full well whose is next
Love me on purpose,

See that I am a monster and stay
Let me dream and prance in sharply awake thoughts

Be a doll, fetch me riches,
Stare in awe at all my clever breaths

Brush and toss my hair, as if it is made of gold,
Create ribbons and worlds at my snap

Show me I can be obsessively loved, too

Language

I love the scintillating sound of 'sleek' on a tongue,

the tip-off of it,

I much admire the words of 'pom-pom' and 'coffee' and 'cup'

Dear skies, the harsh but clean 'crunch;'

The preening showy wisp of 'pretentious;'

The crisp and falling doom of 'devastating:'

They speak like no lover could.

Like they know what they know,

and how to do what they do.

Words are not like me; words are sure of themselves.

See, this dramatic rattle of 'unravelled,'

The soft, slow ribbon of 'unfurled,'

That hawk-eyed glare behind 'peer,'

The lovely epilogue in 'smitten,'

The annoying click of 'tick,'

Or that sharp bite of 'prick'

Words, they are redundantly vivid things;
Say, even 'vivid' is a testimony to the tale,
promising brightness and noise recluse

Allow me to feel alive; watch as I turn death into a metaphor,
nothing more

Hick

Hear, dear, I would dearly hate myself if I was
any other poet;
I know it, I'd read this work and immediately scorn it
Me, I'd scoff, and huff and puff away

Year in, ears down, if I have to keep trudging like this,
Cuteness can count that I'll be sardonic about it

I have creative bursts at the most inconvenient moments,
At the worst of times, the hurst thrashes and crashes old me

I know better than to up and hop into impulses
Well, mostly, anyway, I know that
But the problem is I clearly am a, the, problem

Another Poem About Icarus

Greed of mankind, want for success, shine of ambition:
Blinding and lining the way into the grave
Or so it is told

I am a perpetual, paradoxical 'Icarus'
Ever falling and flying both;
Undecided in triumph or despair, or potential of anything

Sky and water, sun then ocean,
Up, sunned sky; down, ocean doom churned into fable:
Every tragedy is assigned a reason:
All and every, except the one unsold
When does this Icarus get his own?

The ice prick, stone cold, stone dead
Hit, of the waters; of the ties of tides, it
Pushes him almost under but spits out the half-alive carcass,
To dare for more torture
What is he toiling for? Why does this happen to him, he thinks?

So our Icarus says surely,

Surely, of the million things I see and do and am

A something will someday give

And I will see; if only for a second; my sun

But no, no, that tale is not this Icarus

Trapped in between two infinite hells,

Clunking from high to low, bell to bell,

The Icarus here does not get his sun: his own

The sun is far; its knowledge, worse than its burn

The switch between faint warmth and cool breeze taunting,

As he flails hopelessly up then down and back again

And again, and

This Icarus: is he before his time or does he not get a time?

That is the muddle

Poor boy, poor son, the answer is clear:

For every Icarus that makes it to the sun,

A thousand only fall

Without the chance, the warmth, the sun, the own

And this Icarus was never the one for fortune

For high praise, and tales;

Or for the echoing of names and falls in the ocean

What makes a travesty true?

Is Icarus a tragedy if he is more sung than heroes;

If he is considered 'a one?'

Can there be claim to his name as so romantically tragic,

If everyone knows the name and story already

And knows it well

I am another 'Icarus'

I am a no-name no one; the Icarus, the 'one,' is a star

Is this fall a stuck uniformity, is it to not know;

What is my consequence for loving things brighter than I?

Krypton

What's it for a bit of destruction?
That's what I thought when I fell for you
Back when my eyes, wrought, distraught, welled for you
And you let my heart rot in your man-hands

I'll get someone to love me, someone good, you'll see
And damn it all: I'll be great and happy too

What's a trip without an argument;
Why the rise if not, first, the fall?

A thousand cherry blossoms can damn me,
Let a million more lightening rods kiss my rage,
I *will* be happy and great

I feel enormous, I reel unhinged,
Oh, in a haughty and charming way; of course

So you and we are no matter, now,
The latter, the theatrical, bow, is in my company

And she is metaphysically stuck with me
No doormat no longer, no tit-tat, I am soon flying
I have the fight to fight to win

I have the skies, the winds, my hair, my eyes
I'll be alright; if a little chagrin

Soundness

Here I stand, here I thrum,
Withered but unbroken

Born to fight, born to love
What worldly toil can stop my alms?

The quest has only begun,
I am yet young,
I have far more to ruin

This is a yawp of hope
No, the aristocrats won't soon be rid of me

A risk is taken everywhere,
Some dimes are not borrowed

I've been messy with my writings, with my life,
But then so have all heroines of ray tragedy

Rutt

Yelling and yelling and yelling,
How much more rage am I supposed to see?
How much sore can I endure?
Everything a screaming match, everything a war
Everything a patriarchy

No latch presents itself for the damned,
Exit escape and chance;
Scapegoats have no out
Newness is a must but the answer is how;
Only another longing and endless existence spans
One working on and on for the man:

Men don't realize they all know him well,
They'll spurt and swell, unaware,
Scream just to watch the scare;
Look, notice the nonsense.
Men speak as if they are powerlessly powerful.
As if, in their violence, they have no say
Day by day, terror rises for no woman for it is already there

If anything our horror recedes into routine numbness
As often as men guilt with pretend glumness,
See, only idiocy is men's noble heir;
Badness is done occupationally,
Men do anything like they own everything

I have many questions of resurrections
Namely, how the name can still stand;
When men look at themselves, how can they live?
Do they even; they don't act it so
Men make animals of themselves
Then point claws

Stolen Me, Wollen Me

I'll think myself to death
Why I say what I say is a mystery

No more apology
I wish I could save one poem for me,
One hour or one look, one love

Everything I am and have is someone's
My laugh, my mother's,
My sloth, my father's,
My joke, my brother's

If I have stolen my parts;
I am a stolen person, am I not?

Still, I bounce my leg because my old friend did
And old habits do die hardly ever

I'm a fiercer girl now that I am on fire,
But these flames'll eat me whole before I live

Lie and Truth

Liar, how is the truth?

Tell me anything but the damnable

Spin me a tale; not a tragedy

Spill me the feelings and spare me the real,

As you are an artist

I am an art

I will tell what I want

The truth is what you perceive it

Truth is not daring

It is not a herring or caring one

All is a lie, really,

The story lies in the teller, not the told

Who are you to deny fantastical nullities?

Who are you, truly, to stand?

Truth is changing and flimsy,

Not as constant as I

I tell the truth by default, by damnation,

I tell it swell

I tell it well in hell

Truth, how is the lie?

...Actually, truth, how are you?

Do you shrivel in your shawl;

Are you a rewedded thing, with every tongue

Do not answer at all.

Girlhood

Girlhood is unsung destruction;
Who was I before the world got to me?
Can I touch my past, is it too precious, too innocent, too far
Too skewed in my own mind

Am I allowed only to recognize myself
through mens' mirrors?
Eyes, reflecting on nothing, gazed at my formation
Criticized or envied aspects of who I was,
By and by, so much so that I became an unknown
Then they hounded me for that volatility

I am an imperfect vulnerability
I am four years old, and I am nine years old,
And seven and thirteen, still

A girl, there I am; here I am, see,
I am pretending to hate pink,
like it doesn't slather my thoughts and smiles

The adults, the male ones especially,
love to say I cannot understand life
That I am untouched by struggle; I am youth's wife
But neither of us believe that to be the truth; the truth:
Life cannot understand me
Nor more than I can

Go on, tell me things about myself,
Tell me what these bones and thoughts
and pains and curls mean
I'll buy it, I'll believe you; I don't yet know any better

It is painful to just be; when did time leave?
Are these really the same bones? I've broken one,
over the years

I am astonished I can, physically, tear myself apart
It is not long after that I am engaged in a mastery
to tear myself apart emotionally

Before any another man can,
I was and am my enemy and oppressor
and lover and embracer
And how do I justify that? Do I sing my own destruction;

How, on this Earth and hell,

am I supposed to be pretty and alive both?

Optimism and Pessimism

There is sunlight to be found

But it is far and cold and not for us

The optimist and the pessimist wrestle rudely;
First and latter statements,
A contradiction to their heirs

"You cannot exist without me," Optimism says in a baggy air.
"*You* are reactionary."

"As are you and every, any other blasted thing else,"
Pessimism retorts. "What would joy be if no one knew
sadness; would it still really *mean* something? I am your
maker. You cannot exist at all, not without me existing first.

A happy ending would be just an ending without some
trouble along the way."
'People would be bored without me,' Pessimism coos on,
'I am happiness's vital consort.'

‘That is madness,’ Optimism, ruffled, says. ‘A happy ending-’

‘Ah, is one never for me.’ Pessimism states. “In love’s wicked ways, I am a constant. I am the very basis, the meaning, the control. Anything you are or dream is reactionary flourish.”

Pessimism picks its teeth: ‘And we both know I am the better arguer.’

“No,” Optimism simply says. “You are wrong. To even be alive, is to be an optimist.”

Welt

I've melted into the floor,
There is no one here to even understand me
Am I the same girl?
Are these limbs and muscles mine, are they still the same?
Stress is not supposed to be a home;
But, god, what else do I have?
Painkillers like prayers, headaches like reminders of holiness,

Screams like burns of sage:
This destruction is my only religion
It is slow and whistling,
I follow it and it kills and half-kills me,
Why would I worship my own neglect and negligence?
Why would I do any of this to myself?
I cannot focus, I cannot read any of the papers,
any of my own nonsenses
I cannot think; I cannot live

This thing rots by the day and spoils me with it too,
Does it matter that I may be okay,

If all the unknown bruises' throbs and suffering is now?

Dangling okay-ness is just withholding it

No future relief can save me in the now

How can I stick around?

To see only more pain,

To be everything learned: nothing gained

I earn so much to receive so little,

If I am for the crumbs, tell me so

I can throw out all hopes

This ambition is eating me whole

Qualms

How can I forgive myself for what I have not achieved;
I will state this for, lately, I have no answers

Only questions and teas and late night seams,
But this existence is not romantic

I am blurred in academia, in the world,
I offer no clarity and not much rarity or antic

Here, have a part of my heart
It is youthfully dead
I wrote these recent poems in dread,
When I was sixteen and scared
Of life, for life

My vastest qualm is myself
How can I understand this life?
How can I study if I am horrified of being?

I was not raised to be restless, angry, industrial

I was raised to be a wife

I carry it like a nightmare purse,

Everything is a pointless argument in this house

The tension and yells are what I gasp

I am always thanking everyone for anything

I've betrayed myself so greatly, I can hardly see myself

Hist

Whichever came first, my sorrow or my soul?
My bold, unbridled movements are all for borrow:
I fear that I fear too much
And such, clutching pearl and burlap sheets,
I've decided to eat my worries whole
To the lighthouse, to the history,
To the snowy woods in our knocked off cape bay
Yes, coded, there we all lay,
Laymen and seamen and deadman together;
A writer is amidst in the flurry mist, as always
In the rain and vague devastation of it all
If nowhere else
Observer, unserved, the poetry looks upon itself:
The things here are different in the same way
In mysterious and mischievous ways: cannot be achieved
The sea-foam fusses are not to be believed,
In those hands, this eye
These lives are the ugly ones
So everyone says, so the civil wind bends,
So the socialites gag on champagne

And never call it a day

Their spirits slain, humans spit and sing on

A fire that never existed cannot be put out;

Neither can old elopes of miseries

It is a paradoxical hope

To see and live and breathe and accept,

And still live, live, live on

Front

I like to muse myself a tortured genius
As in, instead of only empty;
I simply cannot be sad like a normal person

On the darker days, I see myself atop a shore
A worthless spec thrummed in chaos
And, forever saddens the figure

It's a terrible bore, plain yet maddeningly there in hum

I feel everything in heights;
Who am I to know moderation?
On and on, the extremes swing with kicks

It's a lonesome operation, never having my fill

Is there anything else to say about misery?
It's all been ill-written and played and strung before
My voice is only a squeaking beacon in a grand, greater sea
Can I have a right to these words?

I am asking, can I live?

I am asking

It's always a polite reach for fruit that always grows farther

Farther

At my core, I am lost if not obsessive

I come back to myself like home from ruin

Every day, another toss

East of Nowhere

People will crucify you then cry at your loss
The carcasses of these red, bloody peppers won't resurrect
No easter for the mundane normals,
No forgiveness for what always looks back
What mercy for the Shepard; for the sheep
I should not write foully of the old or bygones
Or have a voice on anything but marriage, they also say
Dead by the day
I grow more into random griefs

My holy rising is no time soon, if it even exists
My poems are mementos to what I else cannot say
Their messiness terrifies me,
New formats horrific
I need no man to tell me I am crazy and unholy
I can do it better and myself,
Bleeding from my knifed thumb and heart
I fear I am my own Roman soldiers
Sword or without
Scratch that and it all, I would be burned not buried

Said To A Mirror

I am trying to love myself

And, my life, I love you and I love you

Why do you hurt me then

How can you live with that, like this

We both know we're imploding,

But I'll let you sit here and talk about the weather

Because you do the same for me

I need to stop living in my head

Talking to myself like I can listen and respond

Who else can I have to question

Four File Dresser Drawers

Four file dresser drawers at the corner of a guidance room
Something about it seems inhuman, big yet cold
These old purple walls are colder,
Everything is odd in a very real way
But this file-drawer set-up,
Something about it is sore

A thing I cannot place sticks out
A thumb pokes out that I cannot point to
They are all different colors, all but two
Except they are more shades or neutrals than anything
A pink and brown fuse, black, yellow yet greenish beige,
and black
It reads like a horizontal one level four piece domino board
The silver handles are disarming,

Just by a bit
It only is weird and off-putting and inhuman:
Just by a bit, just by enough
Enough for what?

I cannot possibly answer that, answer myself,
How would I know
I only observe blindly, clearly
I have no motives for motives
I have no reason for this burden of sadness
I just have to justify it; but how
Poems, journals: in go things I cannot explain
I feel but think about that the more

These dresser-like things all have labeled drawers,
White rectangles with short and
slighted shorthand label stickers,
In bold black ink, that mean nothing
I suppose I need to stop looking for answers in the abyss
I proposition it's okay to be a mess
If I am trying and trying and trying
At least, perhaps

Girlhood continued.

I market myself away from the madness,
I have a sinking hole in my breast
But I cannot bear to look

Girlhood is an ever-bleeding wound and I've twisted its knife
I regret knowing I'm a fantasy,
I revolt at thinking I should or could like it
How sinister to be aware I am wasted before I have begun
How dissociative I feel myself get, and how I beg it to stop
But my brain, my brawn, doesn't listen,
It isn't here to listen

I eat all of my mourning
I did not understand my horror at treatments,
I first did not understand I was seen as an object
I am all of these ages and things and more, all together now

I fear I'll never stop collecting tragedies like high heels,
Do I have a right to my past?

My innocence went to die before I could hold it,
before I had it
There is something men are missing,
There is something they've been trying to steal from me
my whole life
I'm sure of it
I dare not think what a man would think to read this
I am scared of every day, this guilt is not mine to carry
But I cannot put it down
I half-live in their perceptions, I am only free when I am alone
And even then: I do not know what to do with myself

I am disgusted to be warm, to be real
I cannot touch or graze my own body without wishing
it to recede, to disappear
I am light-headed because I am too much
Girlhood, maybe womanhood now, is something ominous

I am not afraid of my obsession, I am afraid of my intimacy
Who taught me this; what is this
I am terrified to be masculine,
to resemble the men I knew too well
I am sixteen
Laying on the gym floor with my friend I do not know

The world I'm forced to live in is one I've never believed in

Everything is narrated by boys;
Do I know myself outside of that?
What is that? When did any of this happen?
Am I dying before I can be, am allowed to be alive

Doll and Ettie

I am classy but sad
A foresting, restive doll made of glass
Porcelain, easy to break yet shining still
The moon over a tornado
A bizarre chaos and small salvation
The unexplainable lies in these hands
I cannot unfurl my dramatics,
Like some old rug or damp dust rag
They simply mold and exist against all's will

Ever Here

I terrify to think I will run out of words
I am supposed to have the world
I am supposed to have life, love, these lies of things

I am not happy, I am supposed to be
I should smile and sparkle:
Tired is the word here
I feel exhausted of burdens I cannot see
I've been it and I'm not impressed,

I shudder to think I am my own salvation
That these bones are meant to carry soul
Nothing much feels like ease
The metallic, brute cranks of my heart feel free and pained
I made it out
I made it out
I made it out!
At the cost of everything
Of my very core

To even the sore score, a lighter epiphany

Life, it hits me, is strikingly similar to music

The pangs and swells, backgrounds and lyrics: the like

Right now, I seem to think I am indomitable

With my mane and shtick of rebellion

I am compulsively the furthest thing from whole

But I am here,

I am here

I am here and willing to love all

I am here, if you do not scare

I am here

If only you would look up

I am writing to you in a quiet rainstorm

And it, like lightning, strikes me how oxymoronic

And dumb that feels

Like it is peaceful devastation of doom

And other pretentiousness

I Write To You

Let me know you, let me hold you
We can dance and twirl
And talk, walk off on lighter things
On dreams

I write to you, always

If only you would talk first
My written word is oath
My spoken one, blabbering and embarrassing
So I write to you

I write to you, always

I could bc who you want,
I could be who you find
On this dank porch, in the beautiful clear day of rain,
I write to you

I write to you, always

In my sleep, I write to you
In my every waking thought, I write to you
On my latest late nights, my derailing cabooses

I write to you, always

My stresses, joys, Mondays and Sundays
And messes between:

I write to you, I write to you, and I write to you

Onto scraps of papers, onto grander manuscripts
You have more love and influence than you know

I may run into wells if ever you knew,
But my silence is still not my sentiment

Rift

Everything, a spineless argument
The tension and yells are all I breathe in this house

I am, always, thanking everyone for an any thing
And all they do is give me histrionics
More troubles, less love

In fact, I am beyond sick and tried of it

If god exists, let him fall
If god dares to tell me I am blessed, I will laugh him to death

If god is real, but if god is real,
I will duel that coward
In all the circles and squares, of heaven and hell

Loose

My goodness and good-will are gone
I don't want to learn anything,
Not anymore
I only don't want to struggle on

Don't talk to me of freedom,
Speak to me of luck

You sit, I'll count
And we'll see who the fool is, fate
We'll see who the fool is, fate

Wisteria

Wisterias, mystery, and euphorias
Euthanize me with ender-pearl eyes
As youth passes by in sweet, pink times
Remember the elegies, the rhymes;
Remember me swooning over all your lies
A romantic is under the weather,
What news: someone call the irrevocable heavens
And plead lavender loves a case
Of ivy, of apples, of the beautifully indomitable vine:
Flowery of wisteria, mist of lost dream.
How do you find it ideal to lie.
So still, tumescent, tumbling
Can you grasp words and wings in stringed sadnesses
The fantastic fews find it unbearable to be,
What views with bones and decomposable glamour!
Throw off the casts of stiff winter, of thick, cold bog
Walk among wisteria's smiles with me
Join the light fog, the lakes beyond the typical tiff
No bitter or gloom taste lingers here
Look, the grass another dewy silver ring

Upon your fingers, up on your crown
Discover the cleverness in sound, echoes, the last
Sear the hot, red sun back with laughs
And maybe, for me, whisper your melancholias

Bird

I'm here to be a brutal poet

I know it

The only discrepancy is I'm shy;

But my voice beats louder at every thrash of my wing

Two desperate, grueling, bulged eyes meet up before the beak;

And break, I vow it, by the day;

Looking and longing before the descent

The world is littered with fake deepness

And the void at my core stirs with its every

encounter of the useless rut

I cannot be one much purified,

Only held down; by myself

Perhaps my formalities haunt me,

Perhaps my own eyes, or twisted hair,

But the culprit is this profound nonsense

of emptiness and pathetic grabs I see

I've come to view inspirational "poets" or quotes as machines,

As cold and dull flowers, as poison ones

Poison to the real poets' tongue

While poets' hearts are nothing delicate, nothing soft

Nothing to oaf and sigh over;

Something to war with, to grapple, to despise at

For poets' hearts are not soft

I, myself, am scant if not determined to default;

if not passionate to peril

The idiotic emphasis upsets me:

As if my work, is their fun and pay

I kneel into every emotion

Except anger

Anger kneads and tosses and flops, chirps and flaps, into me

Keep Up

There is a voice within me that will not stop:
that I cannot keep up with
She is demanding, a fire burning small creatures of normality
An eccentricity and strangeness in the flame
The extent of myself terrifies me
How I primp; glare; never sleep
How my mind is always out to kill the next task for reward
My repression is tender, like flesh
Like mush it shifts so I cannot catch it
Cannot have it to put through and away
Say prayers to the walls, I tell myself
To the dry, standing plates that may better care
I focus so much on polish, on refining,
I forget I am raw and woman
And it perplexes me to think I am nearly grown;
I simply do not feel my own
I cannot keep up with myself,
I am terribly creative to my whim

First Villanelle

I am forced to see myself in every brutality
Of sparks; lights; and hearty mist kept, fogged, at bay
I will love as melodramatics have loved me

A cushy life without any culture: dignity
But willows can wallow on uncannily with the fay
I am forced to see myself in every brutality

While the tossing of things creaks in what be
What likeness to bright spring, wildflower, rain, to May
I will love as melodramatics have loved me

I should not talk of far and further heavens, not me
The skies have screamed to cloud out my any say
I am forced to see myself in every brutality

Every poet mulls over weather because it is insanity
What else is comparable to emotions, in what heavy way
I will love as melodramatics have loved me

My words distort half-like flamboyant monstrosity at sea

Like the purring troubles they rest to lay

I am forced to see myself in every brutality

I will love as melodramatics have loved me

www.ingramcontent.com/pod-product-compliance
Lightning Source LLC
LaVergne TN
LVHW010558160826
845677LV00013B/3175

* 9 7 8 6 0 6 1 7 2 0 3 3 0 *